JAZZ FLU

MB20618
BY MITCHELL KAPLAN

THIS BOOK IS DEDICATED TO HERBIE MANN.

IT SHOULD BE NOTED THAT INCLUDED WITHIN THIS TEXT, HERBIE MANN GRANTED ME HIS VERY LAST INTERVIEW BEFORE HE PASSED. I WAS TRULY HONORED AND HUMBLED BY HIS WILLINGNESS TO PROVIDE EDUCATIONAL INFORMATION AND TO HELP OTHERS SUCCEED IN PLAYING THE FLUTE. I ASPIRE TO HAVE HIS PASSION FOR MUSIC, THE KNOWLEDGE HE POSSESSED, HIS DEPTH AND PRECISION OF MUSIC THEORY AND HIS LOVE FOR MUSIC HISTORY.

THANK YOU HERBIE, FOR ALL OF YOUR INSPIRATION.

MITCHELL A. KAPLAN

BILL'S MUSIC SHELF

© 2010 BY MEL BAY PUBLICATIONS, INC., PACIFIC, MO 63069.
ALL RIGHTS RESERVED. INTERNATIONAL COPYRIGHT SECURED. B.M.I. MADE AND PRINTED IN U.S.A.
No part of this publication may be reproduced in whole or in part, or stored in a retrieval system, or transmitted in any form
or by any means, electronic, mechanical, photocopy, recording, or otherwise, without written permission of the publisher.

Visit us on the Web at www.melbay.com or www.billsmusicshelf.com

Foreword

This book is intended for the flute player who already knows a good deal about how to read music but would like to explore a new route of expression through the nature of improvisation in jazz music. Through this book you will be exposed to the pioneers of jazz flute and how they approach jazz improvisation. This book will also teach you to improvise through the many genre of jazz. This guide will take you step by step through everything from the blues to the traditional styles of improvisation.

You will improve dramatically on your technique and your tone will be enhanced as well. Through scales, patterns and other jazz improvisation techniques you will gain control of your playing. I took all the tools that you would find scattered in many texts and combined the techniques, theory, and history and put them into one big book for your convenience.

I had the chance to talk first hand with some of the greatest masters of the jazz flute. I hope that when you read the interviews with these artists it will inspire you as it did me. I especially enjoyed talking with Dave Valentin, Herbie Mann, and Wendy Klein. It was interesting to note that there was a common bond that they all shared; namely, it takes lots of hard work! My philosophy is that anyone can do anything they want, you just have to put your mind in gear and set it on a specific goal that you would like to accomplish. As long as you have the necessary drive or desire anything can be accomplished. You can do it!

I hope you have as much fun learning how to improvise as I did writing this book.
Thank you so much,

Mitchell A. Kaplan

This book is dedicated to Herbie Mann - One the great flute heros of our time.

CONTENTS

The History Of Jazz Flute

"One must know the history to appreciate where the future of jazz is heading."

Mitchell A. Kaplan

Most authoritiesthought that the history of the flute started with the Chick Webb Group. Chick Webb was a bandleader and drummer who often performed at the Savoy Ballroom. The Savoy was a hall that maintained dancing in Harlem. Chick Webb, as a leader of a big band, supported many musicians throughout the great depression. Waymen Carver (who played flute) was in the Chick Webb group; however, what most people don't know is that Waymen Carver was actually preceded by a gentleman named <u>Max Farley</u> who played flute for the Dorsey Brothers. He recorded with the Dorsey Brothers and the All Stars in 1928. Carver joined the Chick Webb Group in 1935. Although Waymen Carver might have been more influential, Max Farley was the first jazz fluitist to have recorded with a band.

Harry Klee was another jazz flutist from around the 30's and 40's. The next influential jazz flutist came in the 1950's by the name of Frank Wess who joined the Count Basie Big Band. Jerome Richardson, Phil Bodner, and Romeo Penque all played in Porgy and Bess in July of 1958. Sam Most and Herbie Mann were two more very important jazz flutists from the 1950's. Then in the 1960's Eric Dolphy gave the flute new life.

" The flute - all but unknown in jazz until the 1950's. During the past 40 years, most flute solos have been played by musicians wearing saxophone straps - Buddy Collette, Eddie Daniels, Rahsaan Roland Kirk, Moe Koffman, Yusef Lateef, Charles Lloyd, James Moody, Sam Most, Jerome Richardson, Bud Shank, Sahib Shihab, Lew Tabakin, Frank Wess, and others. Herbie Mann, Jeremy Steig, James Newton, Steve Kujala, and Hubert Laws are among the few full - time flutists in jazz." (pg.194) When did the humming sounds start? It was the 1950's with Roland Kirk, Lew Tabakin, Herbie Mann and Steig.

Other jazz flute players not mentioned in random order are: Paquito D'rivera, George Adams, Ted Kurson, Sam Rivers, Henry Treadgill, Art Pepper, Nelson Rangel, Dave Valentin, Joe Farrell, Gregg Abate, Ted Casher, Dick Johnson, Leo White, Wendy Klein, and Mitch Kaplan.

The Flute Embouchure

One of the most important factors to take into consideration about playing jazz flute is the <u>sound.</u> A beautiful piece of music can be destroyed by a harsh tone, or if the player plays out of tune. The position of the mouth (the way the lips are shaped to make the sound) is called the embouchure. This is one of the most important aspects to getting a good sound. Another, important feature which a player must always think about is the breath support. Still another would be the angle, of which the flute is held. All of these characteristics are important to think about while contemplating the idea of getting a good tone. Let's study each of these in depth.

The Embouchure

Again, the embouchure is the shape of the mouth while making a sound in the flute. When trying to get a good sound take the head joint (the part of the flute you make a sound with) by itself and in front of a mirror

*A. put your lower lip just over the hole.

*B. <u>relax</u> the corners of your mouth.

*C. try to push forward with the corners of your mouth (your lower lip slightly out a little further than your upper lip).

*D. blow as if you are shooting the air across the room at a tiny dot on the wall, which would be at a slightly higher angle then your height.

*E. another analogy used is when learning how to get a sound on the flute, one way might be to think of when you are blowing, is to think as if you are cooling off a hot drink with a very even and steady stream of air.

*F. try to keep the aperture (the whole in between the lips) as small as possible.

*G. practice in large halls or places where the sound bounces around the room. This can some times help hearing one self.

*H. Play with moist lips when you can.

*I. As soon as you start to get some kind of sound, attach the head joint to the flute. Always hold the flute so that the body of the flute is facing the right.

*J. Next, try doing the enharmonic (you can do this by blowing slightly harder for a different sound, and not changing your finger positions). Enharmonic is another word for doing the overtone series. The more you do these exercises the better you're sound will become.

*K. Hold out the tones for up to eight beats. This may be hard at first, and may even cause lightheadedness, but keep on trying.

*L. for those who are intermediate to advanced players
and want to improve their sound even more, it is
recommended to go chromatically down by half steps
(holding each note for a 4 beats or a whole note) slowly
extending the range as far you can go down. Some
may have a "B" foot on their flute. My method of
practicing is as follows: I usually start on middle "G"
then go to "Gb or F#". I will then start again, starting
at middle "G" then I will keep adding one more half
step. I do this until I finally reach the lowest note of the
flute that I could possibly go down to. This may be seen
below in example 1.

Example 1

Breath Support

Breath support is not to be over looked. The flute is just an extension of your voice.   Vocal majors will
always tell you how important breath support is. I always use the analogy of the water hose. If you fold the
hose while the water is on then the pressure builds up and very little water is able to escape. This is the

same as your body. Think of your body as being the hose. If you are sitting slouched, or your neck is bent (head facing down) then you will not get the "full airflow" that you could possibly get. Therefore, the sound will not be as superior as it could be. The air comes from a muscle found just below your lower stomach called the diaphragm. This muscle pushes up and the air pressure becomes more stable. You can feel this muscle (and you should always feel this muscle work) when you blow through an empty open round tube as hard as you can. One suggestion is to turn your flute around and blow into the opposite end (this is as good as any empty round tubes) as hard as you can. When doing so you should be able to feel the muscle working. This is what you should feel all the time. Be careful not to over blow the flute. The air should be supported not over blown. It is important to remember that you want a steady stream of air.

The Angle at which the Flute is Held:

The angle of the flute can be important when considering intonation and comfort. Every person's body is built differently; therefore, everyone holds the flute in his/her own way. For the best results, I recommend that the flute be held at a parallel or slightly tilted angle downward from your shoulders. Some flutists tilt their heads, which changes the angle of the flute. Be careful not to go too far with this angle.

The alignment of the flute is also another important factor to getting a great sound. Everything should be aligned the same way all the time! Try to be consistent. This way your embouchure and aperture do not have to constantly adjust to a new position all the time. I recommend to have the bottom foot joint "low C" rod line up to the center of bottom three keys and the head joint (where the hole for making the sound is found) also lined up, so that everything is perfectly centered with the top "B" key. This alone should help dramatically in getting a better sound production.

One last exercise in developing a good sound would be to start off very soft and gradually get louder then gradually get softer again. In music (dynamic markings) it will look like this: P < F > P. Developing your "own" sound is an important and personal thing. You should always strive to get a better sound but at the same time it is all right not to sound like everyone else.

The Fingering Key

● = Finger pressing down the Key   T = Thumb   RH = Right Hand
                                    P= Pinky or Little Finger   LH = Left Hand
○   = Open (no fingers are down)

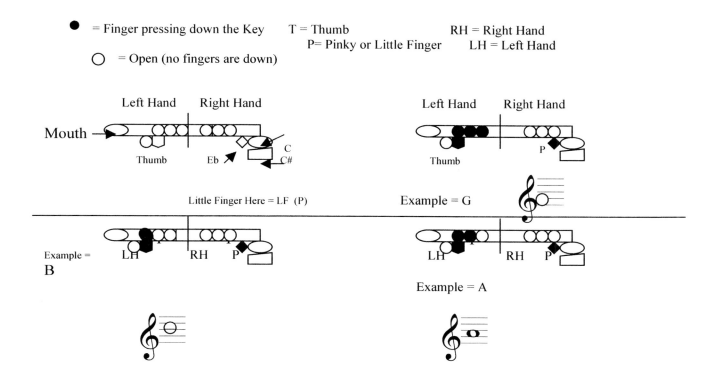

The Flute Fingering Chart

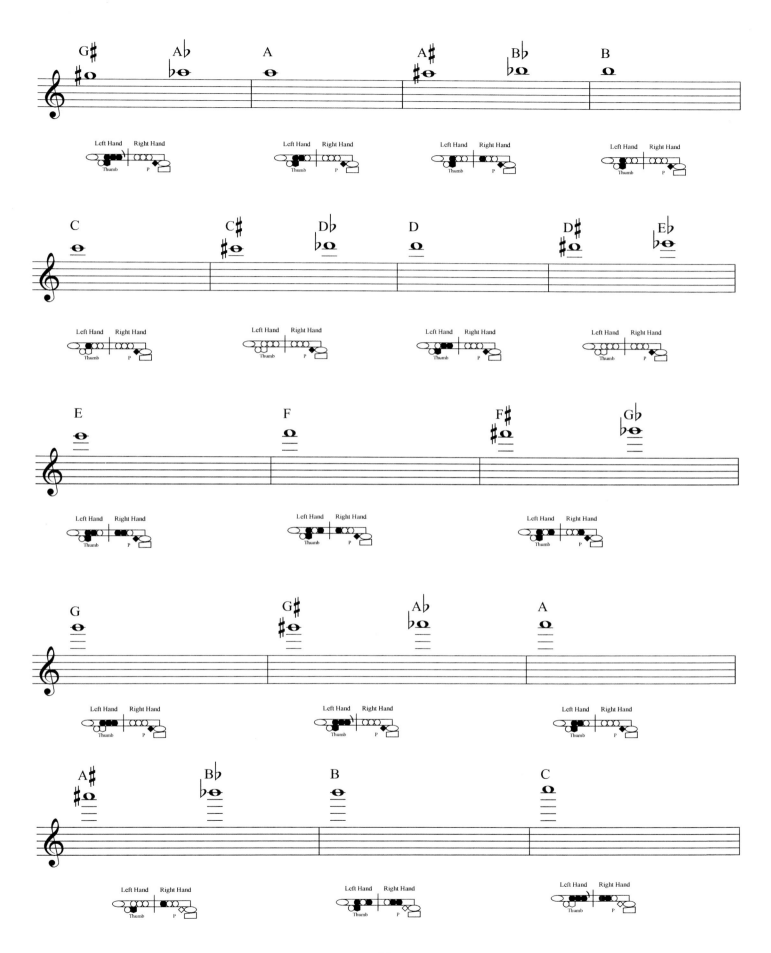

Practice Journal

*Date:*_____/_____/_____

Time: From_____To_____

Small Goal #1

Small Goal #2

Small Goal #3

Large Goal for the Future:

Observations while practing:

Some things I took from my lesson and tried to utilize during practicing:

Comments for my next lesson:

Knowing the Terms

Accelerando   becoming faster.
Agitato   excited.
Allegretto   moderately fast.
Allegro   fast.
Andante   moderately slow.
Animato   Animated.

Beat   a metrical pulse.
Bridge   middle of tune - the "B" section.
Brillante   brilliant.

Changes   A group of chords that one would play over.
Chord progression   a certain order of chords (ex.II V I).
Common time   4 over 4 (four beats per measure/the quarter note gets one beat).
Cresendo   (Cresc.) to gradually get louder.
Cut time   2 over 2 (2/2) everything is half of what you see.

Decrescendo   (Decresc.) To gradually get softer.
Dolce   sweet.

Espressivo   expressive.
Etude   study.

Forte   (F) loud.
Fortissimo   (FF) very loud.
FFF   very, very loud.
Furiosso   furious.

Glissando   sliding from one pitch to another indicated by a slanted, bent line.
Ghost note   (x) marked by an x, a note that sounds like you are playing it but you are not really playing it.

Head   the main tune (go to the top of the song).

Improvisation   to create on the spot. This is done usually over certain chord changes or progressions.

Larghetto   slow.
Largo   very slow.
Lead sheet   a shorthand score or song that may include some chords or melodies.
Legato   played smoothly (indicated sometimes by a slur).
Lick   a small phrase of music.

14

Marcato	a stressed note, marked.
Modes	from Greece, arranged pitches that have a certain sound to them (ex. Some sound sad - Dorian or Aeolian).
Modulation	the changing of a key (usually to a related key).
Ostinato	a short musical pattern which is repeated.
Pentatonic	a five note scale.
Phrasing	a group of notes that are separated by another group of notes by a pause, rest, and breath or by a slur.
Piano	(P) soft.
Presto	very fast.
Pick up note(s)	a note(s) that leads into or begins the music.
Rallentando	to become slower(Rall.)
Release	the bridge of the tune.
Riff	a brief, relaxed tuneful phrase.
Ritardando	to slow down (Rit.).
Scoop	bending (into) the note slightly.
Sostenuto	sustained.
Staccato	short (.).
Suspension	to hold a note while the chords are changing.
Tenuto	to hold, sustained.
Tempo	how fast or slow a tune is to be taken.
Trill	to shake, playing up and down rapidly between two notes.
Vivace	quick.
Vivo	lively, fast.

The Rhythm Tree

$o = \mathbf{1234}$

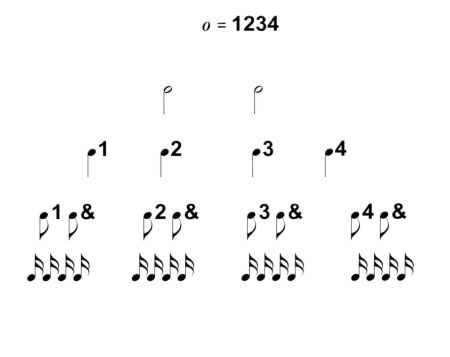

_____ 1E &A   2E &A&   3E &A   4E &A _____

This is a small tree of the break down of notes and how you would

count them. It continues on from 16th notes (which I left off with), to

32nd notes which have three bars (like this≣),to 64th and to128th notes

adding another bar until there are 5. The rests do the same exact thing.

you still have to count the rests just like the notes that you would play.

In fact most musicians would agree that they are almost even more

important. They are the pauses in between the sentences of a story.

They too would have 1 to 5 bars (from 8th note rests on). They look

like this: ▬ , , , , , , , , , , . A beat is when you tap your foot

down then up.1 (E) ↑ & (A) ↓

Learning The Dot

The rule for counting out the dot is:

Add half of the value of the note before it, to it.

Example: As you know from the previous page that the whole note = four beats. You would take half of the four and add it together which would make 6 beats.

$$o + d = o.$$

4 + 2 = 6 beats

---

d + . = 3 beats ↓↑↓↑↓↑

♩ + . = 1 1/2 beats - your foot would look loke this: ↓↑↓ or ↑↓↑

depending on where the rhythm falls when you are tapping your foot.

♪ + . = 3 16th's counted like - 1E& or E&A

Again, it depends on where it falls while tapping your foot.

♫ + . = 3 32nd notes (I also count them just like 16th notes)

1E& or E&A - Except that 4 16th would be on the down beat and

4 would be on the up beat.

    𝄽𝄽𝄽   𝄽𝄽𝄽

1E&A   1E&A

↓   ↑

Phrasing

Phrasing is a major component of performing a song. A phrase is like the sentence of a story. You will have a punctuation mark after it. An example is like a period, exclamation mark or question mark. If there are no punctuation marks in the story you will have a giant run-on sentence. This is the same with music!

You should always try to practice connecting one phrase at a time. Practice the one phrase until you are comfortable with it then add it to another and another, until the song is complete. This is another great way to practice!

So, what is a phrase anyway? Great question! It is a group of notes that makes sense with each other. Usually, it is where you would take a breath, like you would after a period or a comma. As a general rule, try to take breaths after the longer notes of the song (usually longer than a quarter note), or during any rests. Another general rule would be to try to map out where you would take your breaths with a comma mark above each phrase. This develops a rhythmic feel eventually and helps to develop your sight reading habits (seeing music for the first time).

A breath should be quick and powerful, sucking enough air to fill your entire set of lungs. This way, if your lungs are full, you will have the ability to hold your breath for 2 or so phrases.

You can learn phrasing by playing along with other musicians and compact discs (or tapes). Focusing on trying to hear where they take breaths can help you to learn. I find it truly amazing what one picks up by osmosis.

The Dot Exercise

Mitchell A. Kaplan

Phrasing Examples

This is an example from Joe Farrell's Bass Folk Song solo transcription. It starts on measure 47.

This Phrase is taken from Dave Valentin's solo on Afro Blue.

This phrase was taken from Herbie Mann's Commin Home Baby.

Practice Jazz Rhythms

Mitchell A. Kaplan

The following rhythmas are geared towards emphasising beats two and four.
This is a very important charecteristic to jazz music.

1 & 2   3 & 4

simile

1 & 2 & 3 & 4 &

1 o let 2 &   3 o let 4 &

Popular Rhythms Of Jazz

Mitchell A. Kaplan

Syncopation At it's Best!

Mitchell A. Kaplan

Circle of Fifths

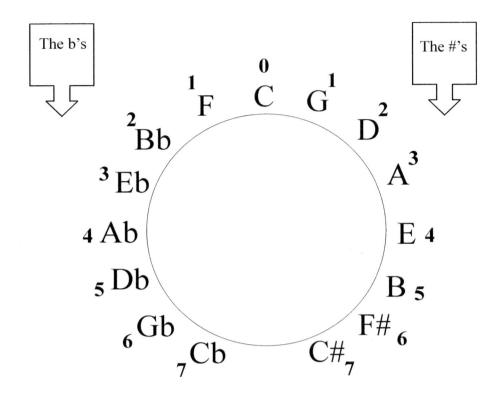

#'s F C G D A E B

b's Bb Eb Ab Db Gb Cb Fb

The circle of 5th's is a tool to create a major scale. Let us take the key of G.   On the staff you would go from G to G, using one # (sharp).   This would be F#.   In the key of D major, you would have two #'s (F and C). In the key of A major you would have three (F,C and G), etc..   Notice that each time you go down a letter around the circle of 5th's you would count 5 letters.   An example is from C (which has no sharps or flats), to G major (which has one sharp {going clockwise}). C is 1, D is 2, E is 3, F is 4, and G would be 5.   This is why it is called the circle of 5th's.   A good way to memorize it is by seeing the word "BEAD".   Notice the names of the sharps are in reverse order.   The last way to memorize this is by writing out a small copy of this and put it in your instrument case. Say it each time before you practice. Best of luck!

Circle of fifths are very important in the world of jazz. I have included a whole section dedicated to the circle of fifths, because of its importance. Knowing the circle of fifths is a key tool to learning all the major scales. Once the major scales are learned, it is easy to progress to the learning of chords. All major 7 chords are built off of the major scales. Simply extract the 1, 3, 5, and 7 of the major scale and you have built a major 7th chord.

Another good reason for including a whole section dedicated to the circle of fifths is that as Americans we are trained to hear down a fifth. Such examples maybe seen from starting at C and going to the key of G, of from G going down to D.

It is also a great way to organize a practice session. By learning "licks in all 12 keys," one can build a repertoire of ideas of phrases to play over certain chords. I have written out a few ideas to help you begin this task. I begin with a two-measure phrase and then go on to a 4-measure phrase going through the circle of fifths. Later on in the chapter of the two five one progressions I also walk you through some ideas going through the circle of fifths. Ideas that you learn through the circle of fifths should be memorized to the best of your ability. You never know when you'll need some different licks that could be used in some difficult keys to improvise in.

Best of luck!

Circle of 5ths Practice Song

This is a 2 bar phrase that walks you through the circle of fifths. Notice the order of sharps then flats.
The circle of fifths always goes clock-wise.

Mitchell A. Kaplan

Circle of Fifths Four Measure Song
In Dorian

Mitchell A. Kaplan

28

Learning How To Improvise

Learning how to improvise can be fun, exciting, and (at times), very challenging!

As Herbie Mann has said, "there are many different ways to get to the finish line." Many jazz artists suggest that improvising starts with your "ears." It is important to listen to as much music as possible and then try to play along. Start with the people who started the trend towards improvisation and work your way up to the present time. "Do your homework," says the great Dave Valentin. Some people say it all begins with the "tune" of the song. That it is critical that you must always keep the song in your mind and work from this. These perspectives are all very valid. They all share a common thread that leads to the "final product." However, it is important to know why you played that "Bb" over that "C7 b9" chord. Improvisation is like a big puzzle. Putting the pieces together the right way is of great value to the performer. Sometimes, it seems as if the person doing the improvisation is just playing what they are feeling at the moment. To a certain extent this can be true. Improvisation is like a "snapshot" of how you are feeling at the moment. A true jazz musician knows why they did what they did. They would have analyzed the chord progression (a group of chords that fit together nicely), and learned which notes sound good to them or which notes flow smoothly over these "changes" (another word for chord progression). Almost every improvisation will be different just as no two-snow flakes alike. This is the beauty behind improvisation. It is a demonstration of who you are as an individual, what you are about.

Let's begin by figuring out how to create chords. Chords are simply the choice notes of the scales chosen to improvise over. These chords are the same notes which the composer selected to write his/her song from. In fact, one might say that the song is just a written solo in itself.

To create a chord we must examine the scale first. The easiest scale to work from is a major scale. There are two ways to figure out how to make a major scale. The first way is by working with whole or half steps. The second way is by memorizing the circle (or cycle) of 5ths.

We will begin by thinking about whole and half steps. There is a distinct order of these to make a major scale. The order is as follows: 1 1 ? 1 1 1 ? . This can be easily seen on the piano. There are white keys and there are black keys of the piano. Each of these represents a half step. If we studied the "C major" scale then we would start on the "C" and go up two half steps to "D." C toC# (or Db), is one half step and from C# to D is the second. This would complete the whole step. With these combinations of whole and half steps (1 1 ? 1 1 1 ?), it becomes much easier to learn how to build chords. A piano is illustrated below to help you further figure out the whole and half step approach.

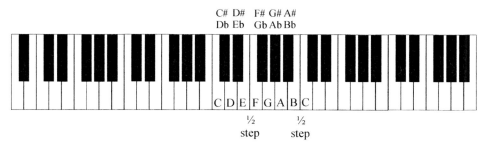

out major scales and to what order they can be found. Learning the circle of fifths will make improvisation much easier. It will shed the light that you will need to begin your journey of improvisation. Once the major scale is put together, the chord can be dissected straight from this structure. Take every other note from the scale, starting with the root (or the first note) of the scale. Skip the second note, and play (or write down), the 3rd of the scale. Skip the fourth note, and play (or write down) the 5th of the scale and then skip the 6th note do the same with the seventh until you have the same as figure 2 below.

Figure 2

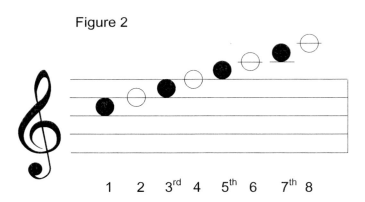

```
1    2   3rd  4   5th  6   7th  8
```

The most common ways to find major 7th chords written are as follows:

C Maj 7

C M 7

C △ 7

There are several other types of chords. For our purpose we will study a few more in depth and then I will enclose a chart to help you figure out the rest. To make a minor 7th chord, simply take your major 7th chord (that we figured out from the above example), and lower the 3rd (scale step) and the 7th a 1/2 of a step. The results for this chord should be: **C Eb G Bb**. It will look like this in figure 3:

Figure 3

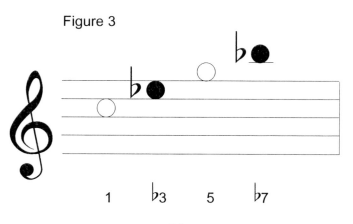

```
1    b3    5    b7
```

This chord is a 2nd, 3rd, or a 6th chord of a diatonic scale. The diatonic chords are every other note, built on each scale step.   The reason why these are your only choices may be because they are the only minor chords of a diatonic scale. An example of a diatonic scale is pictured below in figure 4.

Figure 4

C Maj7   Dmin7   Emin7   F Maj7   G7   Amin7   BØ7   C

Ø   Is the sign for half - diminished.

* In a half - diminished you would
* lower the 3rd, 5th, and 7th a half step.
In the key of "B" there are 5 #'s.
F, C, D, & A. The D, F, & A are lowered
a half step to keep within the key of "C".

The third type of chord that I am going to talk about is the dominant 7th chord (also pictured in the above diagram). To generate a dominant 7th chord, lower the 7th a half of a step. It would then be 1, 3, 5, b7.

This is the 5th chord of a diatonic scale. The dominant 7th chord can be altered in many ways. Some examples would be to add a raised 9th, 11th, or 13th, or lowered 9th, 13th. It all depends on what sound you are going for. You can alter any tones for different colors. An analogy to this is could be; having an artist paint with the certain colors of his choice. Each color brings out a new mood. The 9th, 11th, & 13th are called the "extensions". These color tones bring tension to the sound and would probably be better in the middle of the solo. Greg Abate (another great jazz flute player { more known for his excellent saxophone work}), once said to me during a lesson that, the perfect solo should look like this:

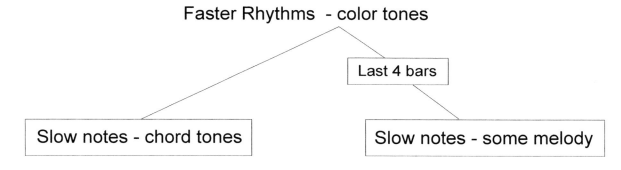

Once you know "how" to build chords, you need to know how to connect them to each other. A smart approach to this would be to play along with CD's that have just the backgrounds already pulled out for you. Jamie Aebersold, Pocket Tunes, Warner Brothers and Mel Bay all have these available for your convenience. Now you can probably down load backgrounds off the Internet. There is some great computer software programs that have become easily accessible. Band in the box and Finale are just two of my favorites to use.

Once you have these backgrounds to play along with, begin by playing the root all the way through the changes of the tune. Repeat this with the third, the seventh and the ninth through all of the progression of the tune.. It is important to listen to each chord tone as you play it through the changes to hear what color it brings to your solo.

After you have conquered this, connect two chord tones together, such as the third and the seventh. Play these chord tones in the same order all the way through the tune. Try playing different combinations of these notes all the way through the piece you are working on only after you have successfully played it through the first way. An example of this could be to take a: II-7 V7 I in "C" major, which would be D min 7 / G7 / C maj 7 and take the just the third and the seventh and play it all the way through these changes. You would be playing a "F" and a "C" natural for D min 7 / a "B" and a "F" natural for the G7/ and a "E" and a "B" natural for C maj 7, all in half notes (or whatever makes up a full measure). Next, you can try the seventh followed by the third in each measure performing it in the same manner. Try different ways to mix up the third and seventh in each chord change. An example of this would be to start by playing a third and a seventh in the D min 7th (F & C) chord then play a seventh and a third in the G7 chord (which would be the F & B).

Once you have mastered the third and seventh combinations try other combinations of two other tones. Once the two-tone combinations are complete add a third tone etc. until you really know the changes of the tune. There are hundreds of different combination possibilities! Write the changes out manually. See how fast you can say them. Take a metronome and test your self. Can you say them as fast as the speed of the tune is supposed to go? Use you imagination!!!!

The Major Scale Family and the Chords To Go With Them

Mitchell A. Kaplan

The Chord Types that can be extracted from a major scale are the following:
C, C6, C6(9), Cmaj7, Cmaj7(+5), Cmaj7(9), Cmaj7(+11),& Cmaj7(13).

Ionian

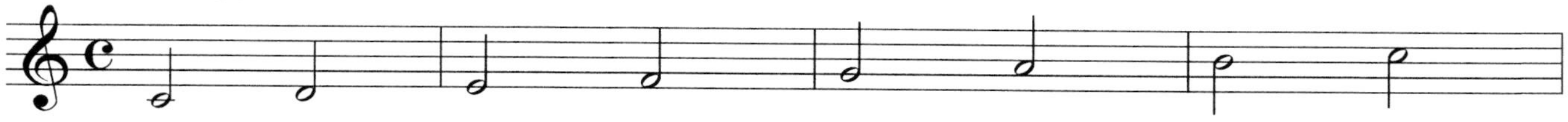

Lydian

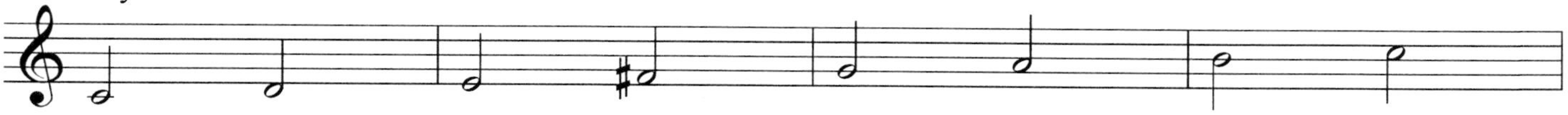

Pentatonic

Lydian Augmented

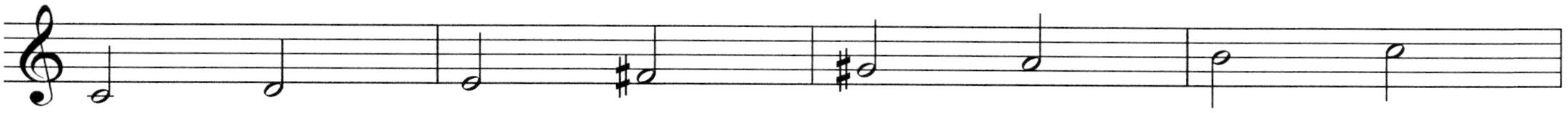

Augmented

Major 7 #5 (3rd mode of harmonic minor)

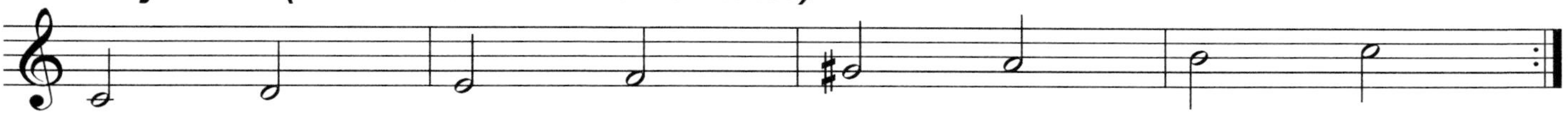

Minor Chords and their scale family   Cmin, Cmin7, Cmin#7, Cmin9, Cmin11

Aeolian

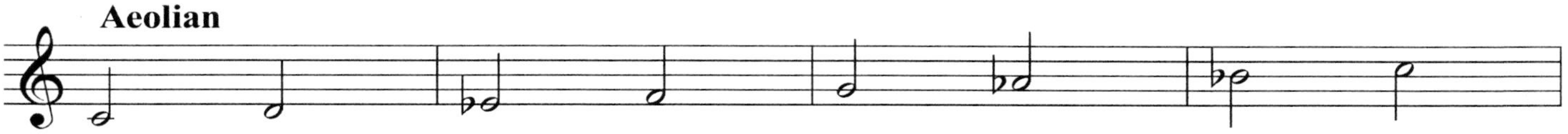

Dorian

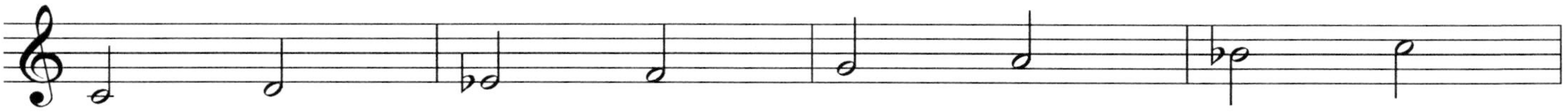

Phrygian

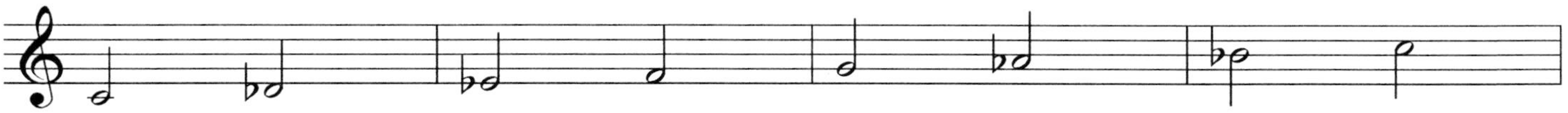

Minor Pentatonic

Harmonic Minor

The Blues Scale Can Also Fit Over A Minor Chord

The Dominant Scales and Chord Family: C7, C9, C13, C7sus4, C7b5, C7+5, C7+11 C7(b9), C7+9

Mixolydian (sus 4)

Whole Tone Scale

Lydian (7)

Half - Whole Diminished Scale

The Blues Scale is an Excellent choice for the dominant chord!

Harmonic minor - 5th mode

Super locrian

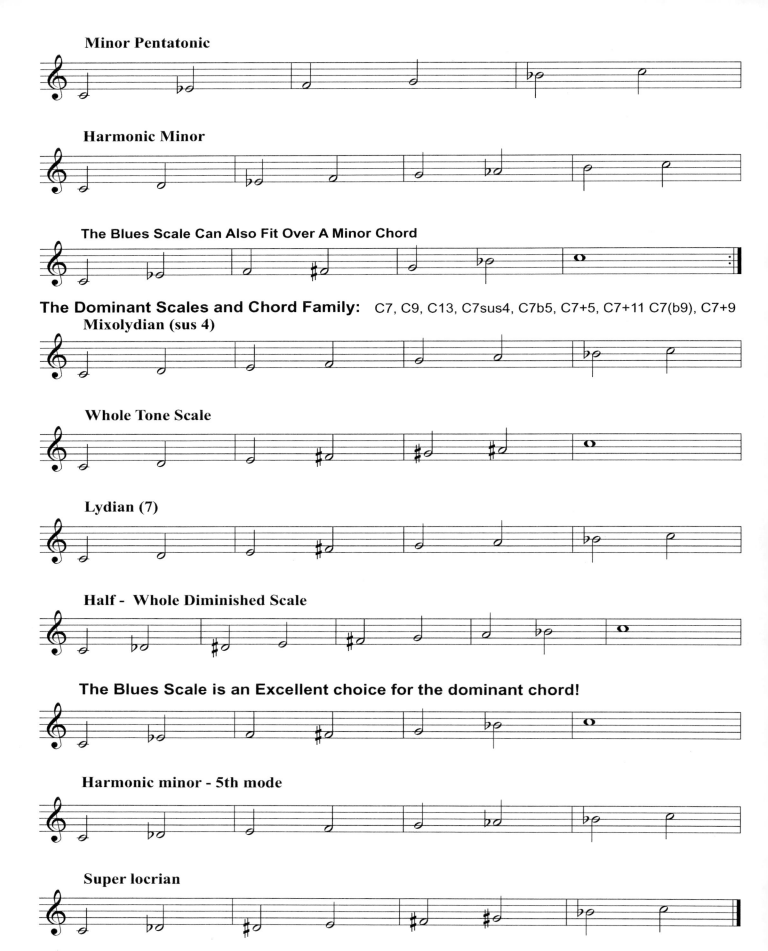

Let's Take an Idea

Mitchell A. Kaplan

In improvisation it is important to use your imagination! A good way to develop a creative flow of ideas is simply by trial and error. Pick a scale, any scale (for now lets pick a blues scale since it is a fun scale to play over) and create a "riff" or a "lick" off of a few of the notes. Develop your riff or idea into as many different rhythmic, melodic, harmonic and other stimulating patterns that you can think of. Let us try one together.

Typical "G" blues scale.

Two measure lick.

You can change the rhythms.

You can add notes to your first lick and stretch it out.

Another fun way is to take a lick and sequence it by moving it around into other keys.

Now it is your turn. Try writing down an idea or two. Take a few notes from a certain scale and move it around. This can be a lot of fun!

35

Using Chord Tones To Improvise

Mitchell A. Kaplan

First, let's try using the third to the seventh of the chord in a familiar set of chord changes. You may recognize this tune (if you can hear these changes played).

Three note pattern using - 7, 3, & 9

Mitchell A. Kaplan

We took a two note pattern and followed it through some familiar chord progressions, now let's take a three note pattern and use the same background changes for this exercise. Notice I replaced the 6th for the 7th when required.

Jazz Flute Etudes (studies)

Mitchell A. Kaplan

When playing the following exercise "listen for the center of the sound".
Keep each note steady and even.

Try playing the previous etude doing the 4, 3, 2, and 1 method. This is when you play each note as a whole note, dotted half note, half note. Quarter note and then even at a faster duration of rhythm.

Flute Etude #2

Mitchell A. Kaplan

Flute Etude #3

Mitchell A. Kaplan

The enharmonics are a great way to develop sound!

Start on the note (like the G which you see in the beginning measure) and keep that same fingering for the following notes. You can do this simply by adding a little more air and making your lips slighly smaller.

Continue on witch the note "E". Extend downward, to as far as you can go on your Flute doing the same exercise.

Jazz Etude #4

Mitchell A. Kaplan

Learning technique is very important to the Jazz performer!
When playing these technique execises swing your eighths. Eighths should be played
as such: long short long short (or _ . _ .). Emphasize beats 2 and 4 when working on
all scales or technique studies. This will eventually help you to "swing" when it is
time to play music. By emphasizing beats 2 and 4, you are taking the metronome
(the small box like machine that keeps the time) and hearing the clicks every time
you get to the second beat or the fourth beat of the measure.

Jazz Etude #5

Mitchell A. Kaplan

43

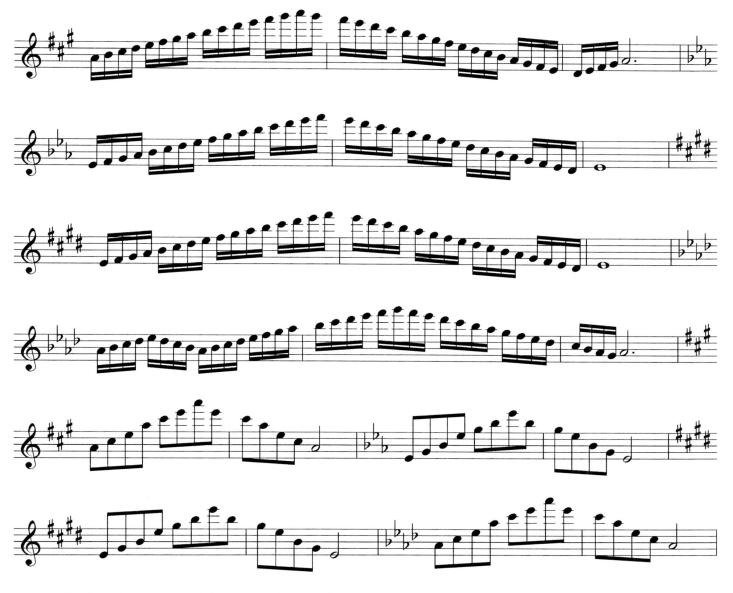

Let's take some of these scales and exercises and mix them up.
Don't forget to "swing". Emphasize beats two and four.

These are very important for breath control!
Do these in every key.

46

Some Harder Jazz Etudes

Mitchell A. Kaplan

Notice the eighth quarter eighth with in the etude.
This is a very popular rhythm of jazz.

Etudes can be fun but they can be challenging! Some of these sounded a bit "outside". It is all right to improvise a little outside using the extensions of the chord or by knowing which scale fits over what chord. The extensions are usually the 9th, #11th, and the 13th of a major chord or 9th, 11th and 13th of a minor chord. You can figure these out by counting on the musical alphabet. An example would be: if "C" to "C" is 8 or an octave then "C to the 2nd "D" = A 9th. From "C" to "F#" is the sharp 11th, and the 13th would be to the "A". The reason why you raise the 11th a half step is to avoid the minor second between the F and the E in a major 7th chord. This is demonstrated below in figure 1.

<pre>
                    9th   #11   13th
Figure 1. C D E F G A B C D E (F#) G A B C
</pre>

One More Warm Up

Mitchell A. Kaplan

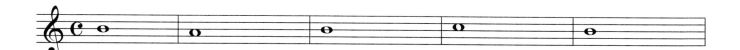

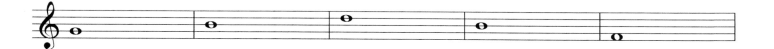

One More Pattern

Mitchell A. Kaplan

The Blues

The standard blues progression is performed in a certain 12 bar order. The order of the chords are as follows: I / I / I / I / IV / IV / V7 / IV / I / I / I /.

What is meant by I, IV, & V7, is that for the first four measures there is a major 7 chord is built on the first note of a scale (let's take the "C" major for example) for the I chord. For the 5th and 6th bars, starting on the fourth note of the same scale, a major 7 chord is also built. And on the seventh measure, usually there is some type of dominant chord, which is followed, by the fourth chord and then back to one, for two more measures. An example of this can be seen in figure 5. It is possible to play a single scale over this progression. This is called the "Blues scale." There are a few different variations of the blues scale, but the most traditional formula uses the following notes of a major scale: 1, b3, 4, b5, 5, b7, & 8.

Figure 5.

The Blues!

Mitchell A. Kaplan

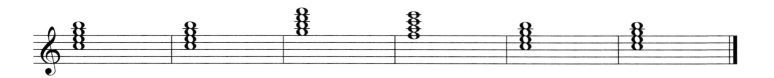

Why Are You Doing This To Me?

Mitchell A. Kaplan

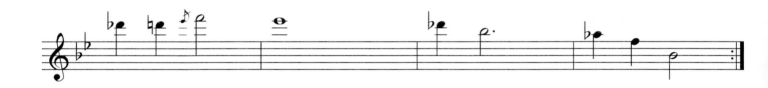

Here is a traditional 12 bar blues written in Bb. What makes this a challenging tune is the combination of speed and higher notes.

The best way to practice something like this would be to:

1. Practice from slow to fast. Take the time to do it right slowly and get it under your fingers first before you speed things up.
2. Play just the highest notes in the order that they fall in the tune. Then, play them, while adding the rest of the notes of the measures. Put the measures, that have the high notes, together with the rest of the song.
3. Play two measures at a time. Keep adding two measures to the measures you can play correctly.

52

Shades Of Blue

Mitchell A. Kaplan

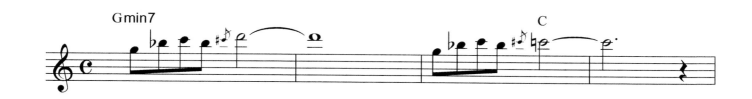

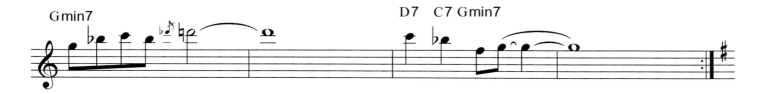

53

Funk In Blue - Duet

Mitchell A. Kaplan

Blues Me Out!

Mitchell A. Kaplan

To Improvise over this, it is possible to use the blues scale. To make a blues scale, take a major scale, such as the "G", and play the root (first note of the scale), lower the 3rd a half of a step (B becomes Bb), 4th, lower the 5th a half of a step (D becomes Db), 5th lower the 7th a half of a step and, then the octave (8th).

It will look like this written out in notes:

Saying It With Out Words

Mitchell A. Kaplan

Some New Jazz Heads for Improvising Over

Mitchell A. Kaplan

Give Me That Funky Old Soul Any Day!

Mitchell A. Kaplan

It Takes Two To Get Funky!

Mitchell A. Kaplan

This song is meant to sound like the 1970's, with a funk jazz fusion sound. Notice it works on dominant (sus) and minor chords.

Mitch's Mode

Mitchell A. Kaplan

Modal Tunes

Mitchell A. Kaplan

This tune is in "A Aeolian". Aeolian is the sixth mode of the standard seven, derived from the Greeks. Each mode has it's own sound. Coltrane and Miles Davis were among the first to experiment with them in jazz. The list of modes in their order are featured after the song. Have fun!

It is easiest to look at a major scale to figure out the modes. The "C" major scale is a good one to look at since there are no sharps or flats, but the modes can be figured out from any major scale. Each mode starts on a different tone and then ends on that specific tone. The modes are listed in the following order.

*Ionian	=	C D E F G A B C
*Dorian	=	D E F G A B C D
*Phrygian	=	E F G A B C D E
*Lydian	=	F G A B C D E F
*Mixolydian	=	G A B C D E F G
*Aeolian	=	A B C D E F G A
*Locrian	=	B C D E F G A B

Try playing around with each of these modes. Write your own tune using each of these modes. Experiment as much as possible. Listen carefully to the sound of each one. Which one do you like the best? Again, you do not have to stay in the key of C major. These modes can fit over any major scale.

Freeze Bop

Mitchell A. Kaplan

II V I Patterns

Mitchell A. Kaplan

II V I patterns are frequently used in jazz. The great classical composer Bach often used them in his music as well. It is an all around familiar chord progression. Here are some II V I "licks" for you to use. I put them in many different keys to make your job easier.

While I Was Talkin   (built on II V I)

Mitchell A. Kaplan

Let the fingers do the walking - Fast Bebop!

Mitchell A. Kaplan

Fire Place Swing

Mitchell A. Kaplan

Peripheral Person

Mitchell A. Kaplan

II-7 V7 I Lick in All 12 Keys

Mitchell A. Kaplan

69

A Second II-7 V7 I Lick in All 12 Keys

Mitchell A. Kaplan

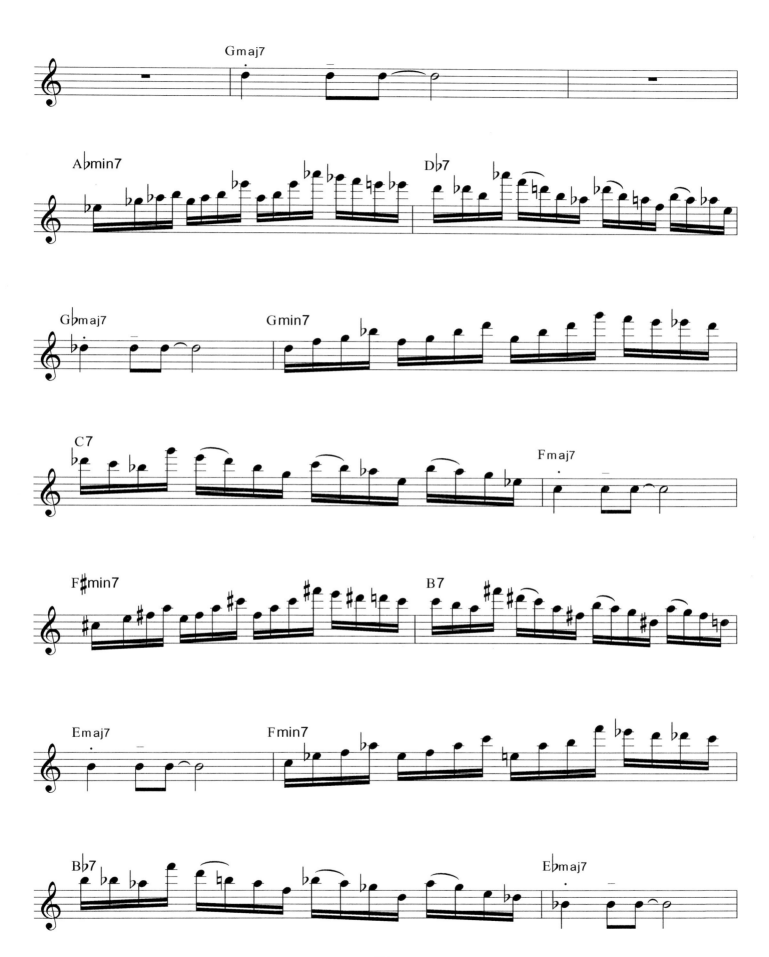

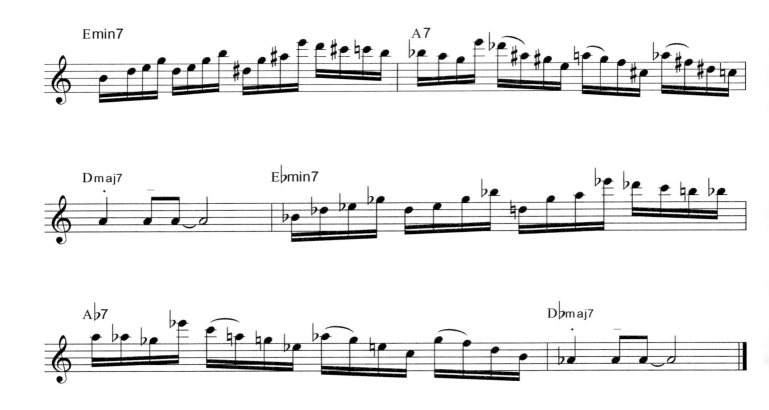

The Purpose of this exercise has three benefits. The first is to get better aquainted with the II-7 V7 I pattern. Again, this pattern is one of the leading jazz patterns that you will find in jazz music. The second benefit may be to develop excellent technique, and the third benefit would be to develop a skill of putting licks or songs into all 12 keys. Putting songs or licks into all 12 keys is very important. One very important reason why this may be so important is that you can never tell when someone doesn't know the same key as yourself. This may happen especially when you have vocalists in your band. Being as versitile as possible will make you much more marketable.

John Coltrane and His Method

Mitchell A. Kaplan

John Coltrane (b. Sept 23rd 1926 - d. July 17th 1967), mostly known for his outstanding tenor saxophone work. He recorded several times using his flute as well. He was a true innovator of several styles of jazz. He developed his own method of "working" a chord. This became known as using Coltrane Changes. The following tune will use these "changes." You can use these chord changes instead of playing over a single dominant 7th chord or a sustained chord.

Rhythm Changes

Rhythm changes are chord progressions that started with the song "I've got rhythm," which was written in 1930 by George and Ira Gershwin (the two brothers). The song caught on and many versions of these changes (or chord progressions) were used to make many other songs. Some of the other songs using these progressions are: "Meet the Flinstones" (from the kids television show from the 1970's, the Flinstones), Miles Davis's "The Theme," Sonny Rollins's "Oleo" and many more tunes by other jazz composers like Sonny Stitt, Cannonball Aderley, Dexter Gordon, And Charlie Parker to name a few. I heard one "story" (which I am not sure how true it is, but sounds right), that Miles Davis used these changes to warm up on before every concert. He thought if he could play these changes, he could play anything.

This set of chord changes is usually played very fast! They are in performed in the following order:

G7 E7/ Amin7 D7/ Bmin7 E7/Amin7 Ebmin7/

Dmin7 G7/ C7 C#min7b5/D7 D7(b9)/ G9   /

B7   /B7   /E7   /E7   /

A7   /A7   /D7   /D7   /

G7 E7 /Amin7 D7/Bmin7 E7/ Amin7 Ebmin7/

Dmin7 G7/Amin7 D7/ Bmin7 E7/Amin7 Ebmin7.

Rhythm Changes Amongst Us

Mitchell A. Kaplan

Licks in All 12 Keys

Mitchell A. Kaplan

Wendy Klein - Interview
Jazz Flutist
Assistant Professor in the CWP
Department (Contemporary writing
And Production) at Berklee
College of Music

Q. What are some of the names that teach flute there at Berklee?

A. Matt Marbuluo and Fernando Brandao (from Brazil) are some of the flute teachers that teach there.

Q. Who are some of your major influences?

A. I came up really loving the word "cross-over artists." The first influence was Herbie Mann and that dates back to junior/senior high school because he was the only one around. Then I really loved what Hubert Laws's offered for Sound, even though it was somewhat processed in the 70's. It was big and his low register was just so thick. I also like the emotional quality of David Valentin. There's Jordon, and James Newton who was someone whose work impressed me, and I tried to study his work but it was beyond me harmonically. I tried to dissect his stuff but it is really dense. He is incredible though, he is truly amazing. I veer towards the commercial dance oriented/crossover kind of stuff. That's just me. I do listen to a lot of Latin as well.

Q. So, a lot of Dave Valentin?

A. A lot of Dave Valentin, but not listening to the people that were sort of parents to him, like Johnny Pacheco. I listened to groups mostly from Cuba.

The First Herbie Mann I heard was with a Cuban band named Machito.

Q. Did you listen to classical music?

A. Oh, for sure! I grew up listening to a lot of classical music and loving it. There are certain pieces by Ravel and Faure that I just love them! And because a lot of people who listen to me think of my playing that I am a little melody maker. I do really tend towards making little songs. Faure songs are simple, tuneful, kid song oriented. The Jewish music in me is really full of freedom. I used to play in concerts at my temple and the conductor would say there is no flute part, just play something. So there was this freedom to fill in and compliment the chorus with my flute.

Q. If you were to give a master class, or if you had to give a speech somewhere, what would you give it on?

A. Try to help students develop their skill in improvisation but through a non- traditional jazz approach. When I was at NEC(New England Conservatory), we actually did a concert where we had compositions or improvisations based on a visual form. It was based on a painting or a sculpture something on the visual arts. We worked on three silkscreen prints that Alan (her husband) had done that he had done based on Christlenocht. Flute, cello and trumpet, we basically sat at a round table, free form improvisation, from this picture (knowing what it was about) and I just remember it was exciting and dramatic. It was an interesting exercise for all of us. To get liberated from playing II V's. To just playing very directly from a visual stimulus. So I might try to think of some exercises along those lines for students.

Q. Do you think that this is the new way improvisation should be taught?

A. Well, I hope the students have already studied their theory, their arpeggio's, they want to get all those physical skills just inside their muscles. I have also done some type of history of jazz flute players.

Q. What are some techniques or approaches to improvisation that you can think of? Do you think linear?

A. When I am improvising, I hoping that I am in a certain situation where I know the tune so that it is really in my ear. So that my ear knows what is coming up. I am a very motive - develop the motif kind of player. If I have an idea then I will try to take it through the changes or I'll vary it through the changes, or I'll see how it sits as a tension on the next change. That's just my tendency. It would be linear, like a composer developing a motif.

Q. Is there anything that you want to add or any advice you would like to give before we finish?

A. Yes! If you come - let's say as a saxophone player to this whole world of jazz. You got people that will help develop your sound sort of ala Sonny Rollins, or ala John Coltrane. You've got those templates of sound. And for flute you've got this raw, unfiltered, unprocessed sound you can hear in, like early Herbie Mann. My advice would be to think about a real voice on the flute. Think about what sound you want. I know what I respond to is when people get emotional on the flute, it's not so easy - you can't push on the flute, you can't bear into the flute the same way you can like the saxophone. I think someone trying to find their way, as a jazz flutist should just listen to everyone that's out there. And find what sound that they respond to. What color you are looking for.

Just a note ♪ to the reader:

The following chapter will give you a brief insight into some of the greatest jazz flute players of our time and from decades to come. These personal glimpses will help you see what they are about and what they stand for (represent) in our jazz world. I feel it is very important to study a great player not by just the notes that they play, but to know the history behind them and to study how they got to where they did by researching them either through the library or the internet. This way you will get the "whole" picture of who they are and what they are about.

I categorized certain strengths when choosing the solos that I transcribed (or had transcribed by Paul). With Herbie Mann, I lay emphasis on his strong ability to play the blues. His solo came from the compact disc "At The Village Gate." With Dave Valentin, I felt I should stress his strong ability to play with time signatures. His transcriptions are from the compact disc "Live At The Blue Note." Joe Farrell; the modal improvisation is very prevalent when he had performed. His solos were taken from "Moon Jerms." Just like the previous chapters, one on the blues, and one on the modes etc. I felt it might help you to listen and study what other great musicians have discovered through what they have learned through their performances.

Master Class

Master Class #1. Is with one of the "first full-time" jazz flute players, Herbie Mann.

Q. Who was the first jazz flutist?
A. "Well, it was Waymen Carver from the (19)40's. He was the first "Jazz" flutist. He played in the Chick Webb band. Harry Klee was also around that time. It was then in the 1950's that Jerome Richardson, Sam Most and myself came out."

Q. Who were some of your main influences?
A. "Miles Davis, Clifford Brown and Art Farmer were the people who influenced me the most."

Q. What advice would you give to aspiring jazz flute players?
A. "Don't listen to anyone else. Try to sound like yourself. The individual voice is the most important. Can you imagine if Charlie Parker or John Coltrane studied with a classical player? They would have sounded totally different then what we hear today!"

Q. What do you think is important for a jazz flutist to think about while he/she is improvising?
A. "Technique and tone. There is no singular correct tone as in classical. Everyone sounds the same in classical. All the violinists and cello players sound the same. It is the same with the flutes. That is why I like jazz. Everyone is different. The student must find what is best for him (or her).

Play along with redcords is one way that helped me to get where I am today. There are many ways to get to the finish line. Again, the students have to decide what is best for them."

"There are many ways to get to the finish line."

Q. what are your two favorite hits?
A. "Well Comming Home Baby was a big hit. But jazz and CD's are just a vehicle for you to show what your life is all about."

Comin' Home Baby

Mann, Herbie, "At the Village Gate," Atlantic records, 1962.

Herbie Mann/Trasc. by Mitchell A. Kaplan

Vibraphone Solo

Master Class

Master Class

**This master class is with one
of the great Jazz / Latin flutists,
Dave Valentin.**

Q. Who were some of your influences?
A. "Well there are two sides to my influences. There is a jazz side and a Latin side. My biggest influence on the jazz side was Hubert Laws whom I studied with for 6 months when I was 16 years old. Other major jazz influences are: Eric Dolphy, Lew Tabakin, Paul Horn, (uncle Herbie) Herbie Mann - it was his idea to do two amigos, the CD and Rahssan Roland Kirk.

On the Latin side: Pacheco, Richard Egues, Pancho Bravo, Marrisso Smith, Jose Sajardo and Arcuno. Arcuno was the "George Washington" of Latin Flute/jazz. His band started around 1914. He was the father of it all (Latin music on the flute). He started the Cha cha cha or better known in Cuba as the Danson. The Danson is the classical influenced, kind of like the minuet. They did not have drums and they were not allowed to play either. So they used boxes loke milk cartons for percussion instruments. Arcano put classical together with Cuban music."

Q. What do you like to do in your spare time?
A. "A like to collect flutes. One of my oldest is from 1833. It is made from Cuban flute wood, which is a black African type of wood. It has 6 wholes and 5 keys."

Q. What advice would you give aspiring jazz flute players?
A. "Start from the seed. Start way back. Listen to people like Clifford Brown, John Coltrane, and Lee Morgan. Be a mimic and be a sponge. Do your homework! Listen to flute players from Japan, China, Cuba, Indonesia and other places from around the world.

The melody is very important. You also have to leam the "changes." Don't play a lot notes. Try to play soulfully like James Moody."

Q. You have played with many famous musicians. Do you have any great stories?
A. Yes, "Dizzy Gillespie once said to me, there are two points in ones life that you have no control of "1. being born and 2. (if your real lucky) Dying of natural causes. in between these times just play great." The other one is by Tito Puente, he said   "If your tired - stay home
If you can't drive - don't
If you are gonna play - play."

Q. What are your two favorite Compact discs that you have done?
A. "My Two favorite CD's that I did was *Live at the Blue note* and *The Hawk*. I liked Live at the Blue Note because what ever you hear is what I did live. I didn't over dubb at all."

Jazz Flute Solo Exerpts/Examples

Columbus Avenue

Bill O'Connell/Trans. M. Kaplan

Flute Solo from "Footprints"

Transcribed: Paul bettencourt

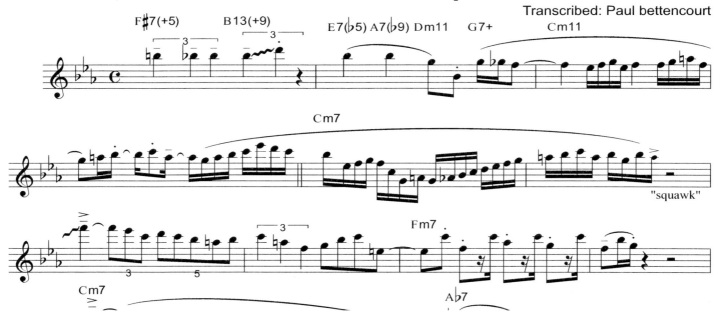

Flute Solo from "Afro Blue"

Improv. solo at 1 min., 29 sec. on CD
(ends at 3 min., 36 sec.)

Transcribed: Paul bettencourt

Mongo Santamaria

(Same chords throughout)

+ These accents slightly "of center"

Music History Lesson

Joe Farrell was one of the greatest flute players. His real name is Joeseph Carl Firrantello (b. 1937 - d. 1986). He started on the clarinet and eventually picked up the saxophone and flute. He was the sideman to just about anybody who was anybody in jazz at the time. He has played with: Maynard Feruson, That Jones/Mel lewis, Elvin Jones, George Russell, Horace Silver, Woody Herman, Herbie Hancock, Chick Corea, Freddie Hubbard, Peter Erskin, Charlie Mingus, and Slide Hampton just to name a few. **Some say that his best playing was on the disk called "Sonic Text" but personnally I liked Moon Germs.**

Flute Solo from "Bass Folk Song"

transcribed: Paul Bettencourt

Joe Farrell

Bright Latin Improv.: E Dorian

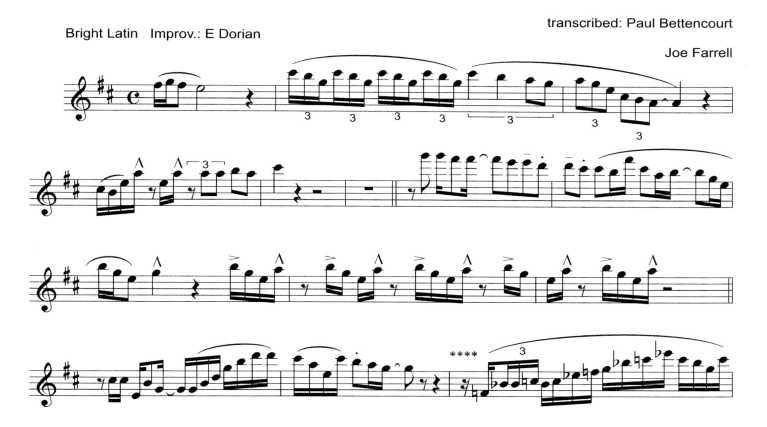

Flute Solo from "Sometime Ago"

Bright Samba

Transcribed: Paul Bettencourt

Chick corea

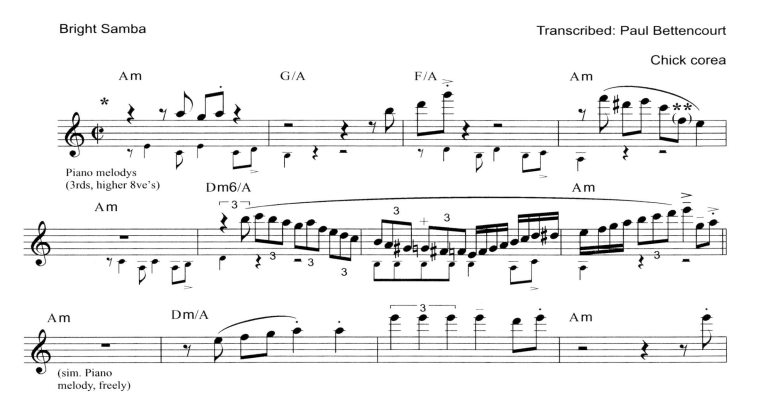

Thank You!

Thank you to Eleanor, the greatest wife I could have ever picked out. Thank you to my son Aaron who is a fine teacher and thank you to my Daughter Rebecca who is a great artist/dancer. Thank you to my dad, Lloyd Kaplan for the music inspiration and mom Sheila for bringing me up to be a hard worker. Thank you to the people involved with this book who have help to contribute in some way or fashion. Herbie Mann, Dave Valentin, Wendy Klein, Joe Parillo, Paul Bettencourt, and to all the people I have had to read over this text before shipping it out.

Discographies

Farley, Max
New York, Aug. 9th, 1928.

Dorsey Bothers
46354-2 VIC21667
46355-2-3 HMV B 5584

Farley,Max.
New York, July 16th, 1928.

All Star Orchestra (Nat Shilkret- Cond.)
400871- B   OK 41083
500021-C

Carver, Waymen.
New York, July 12th, 1935
Decca DL 9223 & DL 79223

Arranged "That Rhythm Man"
USA: King of the Savoy, Vol. 2 (1937-1939).

Decca DL 9222 & DL79222

USA: A Legend Vol. 1 1929-1936

DouglassCompactDisc CX1954
Bodner,Phil
Penque, Romeo
Richardson, Jerome.
New York July 22, 1958

Chick Webb and His Orchestra: (1935 -1938)

USA: Porgy And Bess
Columbia Jazz Masterpieces CK40647

Dolphy,Eric.

Blues The Abstract Truth DouglassCompactDisc CX1331

Farrell, Joe.

The Best Of Return To Forever, DouglassCompactDisc CX372
Light As A Feather DouglassPhonoDisc DMds 4590
Where Have I Known You Before DouglasPhonoDisc DM5629

Folio, Cynthia. (fl / alto fl/ Pic)

DouglassCompactDisc CX3130

Friesman, David
Horn, Paul.

DouglassPhonoDisc DMds

Lateef, Yusef.   Autophysiopsychic,   DouglassPhonoDisc DMds2110
                   Gentle Giant,   - (fl/ bamboo fl/ pneumatic fl) DouglassCompactDisc CX332
Laws, Hubert.   New Earth Sonata,   DouglassCompactDisc CX740
                   Romeo & Juliet,   DouglassCompacDisc CX345

Liebman, Dave. (alto fl)

Drum Ode,   DouglassPhonoDisc DMds 4779

Lloyd, Charles.   (ten Sax/ fl)

Forest Flower,   DouglassCompactDisc CX 7285

Mann, Herbie. 1930- (fl/ percus)

At The Village Gate, DouglassPhonoDisc DMds 3051
Legrand Jazz, CX386
A Mann and a Woman, DMdl 1628
Memphis Underground, DMds 4687
New Mann at Newport, DouglassPhonoDisc DMds 2171
Nirvana, Douglass PhonoDisc DMd1519
Sarah Vaughn, DouglassPhonoDisc DMdl1795

Moody, James. 1925- (Sax/Fl)

Body And Soul, DouglassCompactDisc CX7303
Dizzy Gillepie and His Big Band,
DouglassPhonoDisc DMds 4458
Dizzy Diamonds:The Best Of The Verve Years,
DouglassCompactDisc CX7390
Something Special, DouglassCompactDisc CX389
Summit Meeting,DouglassPhonoDisc DMds5796

Neptune, John. (fl/ bamboo fl)   Bamboo, DouglassPhonoDiscDMds5622

Newton, James. 1953-   Portraits, DouglassPhonoDisc DMds4997

Patrick, Pat. (Bari Sax/ fl) w/ Roland Kirk,   The Case Of The Three-Sided Dream In, Audio Color,
DouglassCompactDisc CX446
Jazz in Silhouette, DouglassCompactDisc CX7295
Live At Montreux, (w/ Sun Ra),
DouglassPhonoDiscDMds A1306

Shank, Bud. (alto sax/fl)   Bazilliance, DouglasPhonoDisc DMds5046
Shades of Dring, DouglasPhonoDisc DMds4607

Smith, Mauricio (FL/ pic/ sax)   Cumbia & Jazz Fusion, (w/Charles Mingus)
DouglassPhonoDisc DMds4570

(Allen, Marshall &)
  Spaulding, James. (both alto sax/ fl w/ Sun Ra),
                            Breaking Point, DouglassCompactDisc CX7626
                            Jazz in Silhouette, DouglassCompactDisc CX7295

Turner, Danny.   El Hombre, DouglassPhonoDisc DMds5806

Valentin, Dave.   The Three Americas, DouglassCompactDisc CX7640

Wantanabe, Sadao. 1933 - (Alto,Sop sax/ fl)
                            California Shower, DouglassPhonoDisc DMds 5320

Wess, Frank.   1922 - (Ten sax/fl)   Carol Sings, DouglassPhonoDiscDMds4154
Count Basie and The Kansas City 7,
DouglassPhonoDisc DMds2254
Opus De Jazz, DouglassPhonoDisc DMdl 1603
New York, 1955 Germany: April In Paris, Verve 825.575-2
On   Midgets

Bibliographies

1. Tirro, Frank. Jazz: A History, 2nd ed., New York, W.W. Norton and Company, 1993.

2. Kaplan, Lloyd S. and Robert E. Petteruti. Who's who in Rhode Island Jazz C. 1925-1998, Rhode Island, Consortium Publishing, 1991.

3. Haerle, Dan, Jack Peterson and Rich Matterson. Jazz Tunes For Improvisation, Florida, CPP/BELWIN,INC,1981.

4. Wye, Trevor. Practice Book For The Flute: Book 1 Tone, London,Novello Publishing Limited,1999.

5. Owens, Thomas. Bebop: the Music And It's Players, New York, Oxford University Press, 1995 (pg.104).

6. Cooke, Mervin. The Chronicle Of Jazz, New York, Abbeville Press, 1998 (pg.130).

7. Rust, Brian. Jazz Records: 1897 - 1942, 4th ed., Vol. 1&2, New York, Arlington House, Press, 1978.

8. Kernfeld, Barry. The Blackwell Guide To Recorded Jazz, Massachusetts, Basil Blackwell LTD, 1991.

9. Feather, Leonard. The Encyclopedia of Jazz, New Edition, New York, Bonanza Books, 1962.

UNIQUELY INTERESTING MUSIC